PURSUING TRUTH & FINDING JESUS

AN INTRODUCTORY GUIDE TO CHRISTIANITY FOR THE HONEST SKEPTIC

J. P. MIHAIL

Written by: J.P. Mihail

CONTENTS

Introduction   v

1. THANK GOD FOR PAIN   1
   "There is No God, and I Hate Him!"   1
   Pain is a Good Thing   5
   God Keeps His Promises   8

2. MINDSET & ATTITUDE   10
   Free-Thinkers   10
   A Winning Attitude   12

3. THOSE WHO SEEK, FIND   16
   You Know What They Say About   16
   Assumptions
   Who is/was Jesus?   20

4. CONCLUSION   24

   RESOURCES   31
   NOTES   35

INTRODUCTION

Whenever I look at *The Creation of Adam*, Michelangelo's Sistine Chapel masterpiece, I see a particular
image. I see both God and man reaching in anticipa-
tion toward one another.

Adam is vulnerable yet made in a divine image.
God is powerful and depicted as a Zeus-esque figure
floating with a band of angels. Yet both have a hand

extended with the expectation that the other will also be reaching out. I see the God of the universe extending His mighty hand in aid of His most precious creation. However, I see something that I think many people miss. I see Adam meeting Him halfway.

How many of us expect God to "sky-beam" into our lives at a moment's notice whenever an issue arises like He's Odin navigating the Bifröst? Our arrogance, entitlement and pain get in the way of what is intended to be a two-way relationship. We end up treating God like a cosmic 8-Ball designed to take the brunt of our anger.

It doesn't matter where you're starting from right now, whether you be an atheist, agnostic, Christian, Muslim, Spaghetti Monster follower, etc. What matters is that you're on a relentless pursuit of the truth and that you have a humble and open heart to receive that truth, no matter how it "feels" when you hear it. You may have had a rotten experience with the "church" in one way or another, but know that the flawed character of "Christians" is not representative of the loving nature of God the Father.

To be clear, my intention for this book is not to demean any other belief system, but rather it is twofold:

1. Help you think critically about what I believe is the most important subject matter in existence.
2. Point you in the right direction with resources and literature so that you can start to journey down this path on your own, but not by yourself.

I could never convince you to lose friendships, be mocked openly and take up the mantle of countless saints before you who have lived and often died for their faith. If I had a sales pitch for Christianity, it'd be this:

"It'll be an uphill battle until you're in Heaven, but oh how glorious that day will be."

Before we begin, I'd like to share a thought from C.S. Lewis, one of the most prolific Christian writers in recent history. Lewis (n.d.) once said:

"Christianity, if false, is of no importance, and if true, of infinite importance. The only thing it cannot be is moderately important."

— C.S. LEWIS

THANK GOD FOR PAIN

"There is No God, and I Hate Him!"

Children often throw tantrums when they disapprove of an answer they receive from their parents. If we gave our children everything they wanted, when they wanted it, we would be responsible for raising a generation of future adults who believe the world owes them something. Sound familiar?

Not only that, if we gave them everything that their underdeveloped brains wanted, we'd be putting their health and safety at serious risk. There's a reason children don't raise themselves. Now I'm not a parent yet, but I have enough sense to know that you shouldn't let a five-year-old play with a blender.

When God doesn't answer prayer the way we want and when we want, do we act like a cranky toddler, or are we able to reflect and acknowledge that our emotional and momentary desires might not ultimately be good for us? We might think that we're simply diving into an inconspicuous pond, but God sees the creatures and jagged rocks waiting under the water's surface that we're oblivious to. According to Christian doctrine, God is an all-powerful and all-knowing Heavenly Father, which means that He sees far beyond the scope of our limited understanding. With that in mind, does it not make sense to acknowledge the fact that He would therefore know best? Putting our trust in God's will for our lives is akin to putting our faith in our parents as children.

Unfortunately, many people don't have healthy parental role models who can paint an image of God as "Father," which leads me to my next point. Most opinions against God that I've come across over the years end up sounding something like this...

"There is no God, and I hate him!"

Now, does that sound reasonable, or does it sound like it's coming from a place of hurt? A father-wound often leads to very damaging behaviours. If the statistics from the image on the next page aren't heartbreaking enough, imagine what a fatherless home would do to one's perception of God being your loving, Heavenly "Father."

MAYBE YOU DON'T HAVE to imagine.

THE FATHER ABSENCE CRISIS IN AMERICA

There is a crisis in America. According to the U.S. Census Bureau, 18.3 million children, 1 in 4, live without a biological, step, or adoptive father in the home. Consequently, there is a "father factor" in nearly all of the societal ills facing America today. Research shows when a child is raised in a father-absent home, he or she is affected in the following ways...

Source: U.S. Census Bureau. (2020). Living arrangements of children under 18 years old: 1960 to present. Washington, D.C.: U.S. Census Bureau.

POVERTY

4X GREATER RISK OF **POVERTY**

TEEN PREGNANCY

7X MORE LIKELY TO BECOME **PREGNANT AS A TEEN**

BEHAVIORAL PROBLEMS

MORE LIKELY TO HAVE **BEHAVIORAL PROBLEMS**

CHILD ABUSE

MORE LIKELY TO FACE **ABUSE AND NEGLECT**

MOM-CHILD HEALTH
2X GREATER RISK OF **INFANT MORTALITY**

SUBSTANCE ABUSE

MORE LIKELY TO ABUSE **DRUGS AND ALCOHOL**

INCARCERATION
MORE LIKELY TO GO **TO PRISON**

CHILD OBESITY

2X MORE LIKELY TO SUFFER **OBESITY**

CRIME

MORE LIKELY TO **COMMIT CRIME**

EDUCATION

2X MORE LIKELY TO DROP OUT **OF HIGH SCHOOL**

Pain is a Good Thing

I recently heard a story about a girl who had Congenital Insensitivity to Pain (CIP). People afflicted with this condition could have their hand on a stovetop and not feel the bubbling, melting flesh until it's too late. They could even have cuts become infected because they never tended to the wound they weren't aware they had. It might sound cool not to feel pain, but it's quite the opposite; it's hazardous.

To sum up the story, the girl's mother prayed every night, asking God to let her baby feel pain. Can you imagine asking for such a thing? It almost sounds sadistic on its face. I wanted to discuss this topic in the first chapter because it seems to be one of the biggest hindrances for many new Christians and anyone pursuing Christianity.

"If God is SO good, then why... *insert trauma here*?"

Have you ever asked that yourself? We often forget how vital pain is to the growth process and how essential it is to survive. Your muscles don't grow without resistance, and a sword can't be forged without fire and blunt force trauma. Life is a gauntlet of trials, but if you approach that gauntlet wondering why everything is happening **TO** you, then you're probably going to come out of each event weaker and more beaten down than the last. This mindset is often referred to as a "victim's mentality," and most people don't realize that it is 100% a choice.

On the other hand, if you view those same trials as an opportunity for growth, with the attitude that life is happening **FOR** you rather than **TO** you, chances are you will come out the other side of that gauntlet stronger and more resilient. If you can learn to become grateful for the trials, you can start to live a life of gratitude with a positive attitude and not give your power away to the enemy every time something goes wrong.

God doesn't always interfere, but He is always in control. God is a loving Father, not an abusive master, and as a father, sometimes He sees things that we don't. Although it hurts His heart to see us suffer, just like that mother who prayed for her daughter to feel pain, sometimes God needs to let us feel pain to save us from a greater sorrow. To be clear, this does **NOT** mean that God is the one inflicting the pain. It simply means that He often allows things to happen, although we may not understand why in our grief.

If we're honest, our pain is often a direct result of our own poor choices. We need to learn to accept greater responsibility for our actions and our attitudes so that we're not always pointing the finger at everything and everyone but the culprit; ourselves. My intention is not to condemn or make you feel guilty but to help you realize that your biggest stumbling block could very well be yourself. Trust me, it's not an easy pill for anyone to swallow, including myself.

ONE DAY while in the 4th grade, I was bouncing a pencil on its eraser at my desk. Out of nowhere, the teacher spoke up with an announcement for the class, and as I expediently looked up towards her, I didn't realize that my pencil was still mid-bounce. Like a good student, I rapidly placed my arms down on my desk and was greeted with an unpleasant sensation. The resulting pencil hanging by the graphite tip out of my wrist was a traumatizing moment, to say the least. Thankfully it didn't lodge itself too deep, but I've had a tiny black dot on my wrist ever since. Let's just say I became warier around sharp objects after that lesson, but I never blamed God for stabbing me.

God Keeps His Promises

The God of the Bible, by His very nature, is outside of space and time since He ultimately created space and time. Because our perception of time is so finite, it can be challenging for us to accept that God sees our past, present and future in the same instant. He is infinite. We are finite.

What might seem impossible for you to bear right now may be the very catalyst that God will use to prevent thousands from taking their own lives someday. God will always provide comfort and peace for those who love Him and trust in His will. That is a promise made time and time again throughout scripture.

Candy Lightner was a housewife and mother, and by American standards, lived a "typical" life. Everything changed in 1980 when her 13-year-old daughter was killed in a drunk driving accident by a man with multiple previous DUI incidents on record. Candy's pain could've led her to a life of isolation and sorrow. No one would have blamed her. Instead, she decided to partner with a handful of other mothers who had undergone similar tragedies to form the organization known as MADD or Mothers Against Drunk Driving. To date, the efforts of MADD have saved approximately 330,000 lives in the USA alone and have played a pivotal role in progressing legislation surrounding impaired driving in North America (MADD, n.d.).

I LOVE the notion that pleads,

"Don't waste your pain."

Instead of being the fire that consumes you, understand that it can be the furnace that forges you. I hope that the foggy lens you may be looking through can be wiped clean with the cloth of truth. Don't let your pain stand in the way of your relationship with your Heavenly Father any longer. You still might not fully believe in God, but my friend, know that He believes in and loves you unconditionally.

2

MINDSET & ATTITUDE

Free-Thinkers

My mentors taught me to be a free-thinking person in all areas of my life. What does that mean, you might be asking? Good question!

If you had a goal to become the greatest boxer of all time, you'd want access to a coach like Cus D'Amato, if he was still alive, Mike Tyson's old coach. I think that's a fair statement.

Now let's say your cousin, uncle, friend's mother, or the mailman decide to tell you what they think about your technique and your training regimen. Whose opinion will hold more weight in your mind, your expert coach or your friend/relative who has no professional boxing experience? Now, this doesn't mean those people aren't trying to help you genuinely, but opinions are like armpits. Everyone has a couple, and they usually stink.

A free-thinking man or woman is intentional about whom they allow to speak into their life and from what sources they accept their information. The question that we all need to ask ourselves while on a knowledge and truth quest is:

Who am I listening to and why?

If you go to Google right now and type in, "Mother Theresa was a Satanist," I can promise that you'll find quite a few results. Now, why would you ever write something so preposterous into an online search engine, you may be thinking? Oh, I don't know, for the same reason that people are typing in things like, "is Christianity a cult?" "Will my dog go to heaven?" "Are *E.T.* and *Star Wars* actually in the same universe?"

People typically want to find one of two things: information or confirmation.

If it's not already clear, I encourage you to be an information seeker, not just someone who seeks to confirm their current biases. Be wary not to be so saturated in your tradition and current belief systems that you miss the truth itself when it inevitably slaps you across the face. The road to hell is paved with good intentions, after all. There are unfortunately a lot of "good people" who believe they're on the yellow brick road, but wide is the "Highway to Hell" and narrow is the "Stairway to Heaven."

A Winning Attitude

If you're a reasonable person, you're probably nodding your head to most of what I've written so far in this chapter; however, you're probably wondering how to apply what I've just discussed. Where do I go, and whom do I listen to? Fear not, my friend!

The best part of this entire book will be the catalogue of resources that I have included in the "**Resources**" section at the end. I hope you'll enjoy my writing, but I know that the only reason I'm even able to put together a short book like this for you is because of the wisdom and knowledge that I've gleaned over the years from wiser men and women and ultimately from God Himself.

I want to share some Olympic-level mindset with you right now, and it's going to be intense... are you ready?

Follow Through.

All kidding aside, if you are on a mission, if you have a goal to uncover the real Jesus Christ and if you want truth at all costs, then you have to, I repeat, **HAVE TO** be willing to do the work. You can't go to the gym twice a month and eat cake every day and expect a six-pack. Likewise, you can't simply watch a two-hour documentary on Netflix and claim that you've "looked into" Christianity and that "Jesus guy." Let's be intellectually honest and philosophically consistent. Laziness never saved a princess or won a gold medal.

One of the first things I encourage you to do after reading this book is to watch the movie named after the best-selling book by Lee Strobel, *The Case for Christ (2017)*. The film is a fantastic representation of a real man's journey to disproving Christianity. The book goes into a considerable amount of evidentiary detail based on all the findings Lee Strobel uncovered in his relentless pursuit to dethrone the "God-man" and the "cult of Christianity." Still, the movie is a great starting point for most people. Not only will the contents of Lee Strobel's book and subsequent film provide an excellent starting point, but I believe it will give you a good idea of what it looks like to be a true skeptic in pursuit of the truth.

A little-known fact about the great C.S. Lewis, who penned many works, including the infamous *Chronicles of Narnia*, is that he too had a rocky journey from faith to atheism and back to faith in Christ. A powerful quote from Lewis' book, *Mere Christianity (1952, pp. 45-46)*, explains a little bit of his journey:

"My argument against God was that the universe seemed so cruel and unjust. Just how had I got this idea of just and unjust? A man does not call a line crooked unless he has some idea of a straight line. What was I comparing this universe with when I called it unjust? ... Thus, in the very act of trying to prove that God did not exist—in other words, that the whole of reality was senseless—I found I was forced to assume that one part of reality—namely my idea of justice—was full of sense. Consequently,

atheism turns out to be too simple. If the whole universe has no meaning, we should never have found out that it has no meaning."

— C.S. LEWIS

J.R.R. Tolkien was a close friend to Lewis. Their relationship played a pivotal role in Lewis coming back to faith in Christ. Just as Tolkien inspired Lewis, Lewis encouraged and inspired Tolkien to publish his great works, a little-known series called *The Hobbit* and *The Lord of the Rings* (Carter, 2017). A little trivia never hurt anybody, am I right?

It's okay to be a skeptic; just make sure that you're an honest one. Ask challenging questions and do your due diligence. If you want to live a life of me, myself and I and have no room for any greater calling, belief or purpose; then you're free to do so.

Just remember that Newton's Third Law of Motion applies to your life as well as physics. For every action, there will be an equal and opposite reaction.

Everything you do has a consequence, whether you like it or not. Some actions have consequences that just happen to be eternal.

3

THOSE WHO SEEK, FIND

You Know What They Say About Assumptions

At this point, you might be thinking, "when is he going to get to the point?" If that's the case, then I'd argue you're already missing it. We live in the 21st century and have Google in our pockets, so you don't have a lack of access to information (at least if you live in the West); you may just have a hardened heart. You might not want the Bible to be true.

Now don't get me wrong, the fact that you're even reading this is a great thing, all I'm saying is that you need to learn, accept and practice the fundamentals before you start beating everyone at the park in chess.

On the other side of things, if you're reading this with a very open heart and mind but don't know where to start in your educational journey because the amount of information available to you is so vast, then keep reading because I'm here to help!

I titled this chapter "Those Who Seek, Find" because it seems to be the case throughout history that whenever a skeptic approaches the topic of disproving Christianity, they always fall up short and are never able to "disprove" anything the Bible claims with absolute certainty. You might be thinking that I'm a fool because science has proven the Bible wrong time and time again! False.

Science doesn't say anything; scientists do.

Did you know that most of what we teach as "scientific facts" about the Earth's core is all an assumption? We physically cannot penetrate the Earth's surface deep enough to know beyond a reasonable doubt what the planet's innermost layers actually look like. The Earth supposedly extends 6,400 km below our feet, yet we've only drilled approximately 12 km into its surface (Geiger, 2019).

Now, this particular fact has nothing to do with Christianity (clearly), but frankly, I just find it fascinating that most people reading this will probably think to themselves, "Huh... no kidding, eh?" I know I did.

If the scientific evidence was so abundantly clear that the Bible is false, why are there still Christian scientists/physicists/historians/geologists/etc.? They would be absolute morons to deny blatant and objective truth, right? Data needs to be interpreted. Unfortunately, biased people with preconceived ideas about the universe and God's existence often interpret the data in a... you guessed it, biased manner.

Many observable natural processes can verify micro-evolution, such as adaptation to one's environment, natural selection or "survival of the fittest," mutations, etc.

Not once, however, have we observed macro-evolutionary claims such as one species morphing into an entirely new species or the creation of something from nothing as indicated by the Big Bang **THEORY.**

Don't get me wrong, most of the assumptions we make are based on compelling and logical evidence. I'm simply stating that we need to recognize that even Darwin and everyone after him still call it the "theory" of evolution, not the "fact" of evolution.

Now the purpose of this particular book is not to take a deep dive into the evidence for Christianity or get all "science-y" on you. My intended purpose is to prepare and equip you to pursue that knowledge through the sources that I will list at the end of this short book.

Many religious opponents will talk about the fact that Christians just put their faith in the writings of a bunch of so-called "dead men" whom they've never met, and I would argue that most atheists and non-believers do the same.

Let's be honest. Most of us have not studied astrophysics, microbiology, cosmology, or any related advanced field of study. Most people just regurgitate what they've heard from intellectuals they put their faith in even though they've never met them. Let's be even more honest; some of us just heard it on social media, on TV, or from a coworker and took it as fact without any due diligence.

Why do you believe what you believe? Have you seen the data for yourself? Do you know personally or trust the politicians, scientists, doctors, etc. who present the evidence to you?

A great resource for you to dive into these kinds of questions is to follow "Cross Examined Ministries" on YouTube and any podcasting platform you use.

Frank Turek and Norman Geisler's book, *I Don't Have Enough Faith to Be an Atheist*, would be a fantastic scholarly supplement to those videos as well.

Who is/was Jesus?

Okay, so who was Jesus Christ of Nazareth? Was He even real?

In short, yes.

Jesus Christ is the most well-documented historical figure in all ancient literature, hands down. The New Testament documents are the most reliable, accurate and abundantly available literary works in all the ancient world. The evidence is astounding by every metric. Not to mention our entire Western calendar is based on His life and death. B.C. stands for "before Christ," and A.D. stands for "anno domini" in Latin which translates to "in the year of the Lord" (Coolman, 2014). Would we base our historical timeline on a fictional character? I think not.

Jesus was most certainly a real man. However,

you'll hear a lot of non-believers and other religious folk say something along the lines of,

"He was a good man and maybe even a prophet, but I don't believe He is who He claimed to be (AKA God incarnate)."

Okay, let's think about that and break it down a little bit. If Jesus was not who He claimed to be, then He was most certainly a bastard child born out of wedlock at a time and place in history where His mother could've been stoned to death for such a crime. He was a homeless carpenter that hung out with twelve other intentionally homeless wandering men. He always got Himself in a tiff with the local religious authorities. He vandalized a temple. He claimed to be GOD Himself, which even Elvis didn't do... I think you get the point.

This guy was a raging lunatic and probably deserved to be put to death for blasphemy and anarchy... IF... He was not who He claimed to be.

Now I believe you have to ask yourself if a homeless lunatic who claimed to be the literal God of the universe would be able to do the following:

1. Perform the miracles recorded in the New Testament and other ancient writings;

2. Persuade one of Christianity's greatest persecutors, Saul of Tarsus, to renounce his religion and become the Apostle Paul, one of Christianity's greatest martyrs and church fathers who ever lived;

3. Persuade almost every single one of His apostles to allow themselves to be stoned to death, crucified, burned alive, beheaded, etc. for what they would have known to be an absolute lie;

4. Persuade thousands of early Christians to be lit alive on the streets of Rome as "Roman Candles," or thrown into Nero's games where they would be torn apart and eaten by animals for amusement;

5. Persuade countless Christians over the last 2000 years to willingly give their lives for their faith across the entire globe; and

6. Change the hearts and lives of millions of people still today over two millennia later.

For these reasons and many others I won't list in this short book, is it truly acceptable to say that Jesus was just a "good man?" Is it reasonable to say that He was a nut case?

I think it's fairer to say that maybe He was who He said He was, as impossible as that might sound. The empty tomb is a historical fact. The only question is, where did the body go, and who moved it?

4

CONCLUSION

I choose to believe that Christ is who He said He was.

THAT IS a big decision that only you can make for yourself. Every man or woman who honestly walks down this road is going to find answers. The question is, what answers do you want to find and are you willing to accept what you discover?

If you conclude that Jesus is the Son of God and that Christianity is indeed the truth, then you're accepting quite a few things along with it by default.

1. Other religions are false
2. There truly is only one way to Heaven

3. The New & Old Testaments are true
4. Jesus died for your sins
5. You are now responsible and accountable for your actions and your decisions
6. There is an objective moral standard outside of yourself

That's just a few off the top of my head, for starters.

Now that doesn't mean that you need to change your life or do anything different. You can accept the truth and then do nothing about it; that's your choice. Just understand that your choice now has eternal consequences.

I'm going to leave you with a comprehensive list of materials to begin your journey in the "**Resources**" section of this book, just a few pages forward. I'll list titles of books, movies, YouTube channels, speakers, and more, that have radically impacted my life personally and that I know will help you as a truth seeker find the knowledge and wisdom you need to go and grow.

I want to leave you with one last illustration of God's love for you, and I want to thank you for reading through this short book. I genuinely hope that I've touched your heart in some way through my words. I give all credit to God if so.

If you would be so kind as to leave an honest rating on this book's Amazon page, it would help this ministry tremendously so that others may read and be exposed to the contents in this book. God bless you my friend!

A BOY LOVES A GIRL.

He wants her to be his bride. Throughout her life, he pursues her, writes her love letters, leaves her voicemails, and longs for an intimate relationship with her. Unfortunately, as the girl gets older, she rejects the boy's love, and that rejection ultimately turns into resentment. She tries to block his number, change addresses, and does whatever she can to get him to leave her alone. She eventually succeeds and is left to live her life the way she wants to without the boy's interference any longer.

Years pass by, and one day without expectation, the girl loses consciousness. She wakes to find herself tied to a chair in a place she doesn't recognize. A figure walks up to her and turns on a light. It's... the boy from her youth.

He says to her, "Aren't you happy? We're together at last, and nothing can keep us apart anymore! I love you."

LET'S just pause for a moment.

Do you feel uncomfortable right now? I know I do even writing this. Love can never be forced. By its very nature, it must be given freely. The girl will never truly love the boy now since he's removed free will from the equation.

This illustrates what it would be like if God forced everyone into Heaven when they died. Our time on this Earth is our opportunity to pursue a relationship with our Creator. If we reject him our entire lives here, then God loves you too much to force you to be with Him for eternity. It might not make sense at first glance but read this slowly.

God loves you so much that He would never force you to be in His presence for eternity when you've rejected His love your entire life.

You and I didn't ask to be created, but we were. So how can God send us to Hell when we didn't even ask to be here? Hell wasn't designed for you and I, my friend. It's intended for the Devil and his angels.

However, if you knowingly reject God's love now, the only place that will exist outside of His presence will be Hell, a place where you are not designed to reside.

My prayer for you is that you will learn to humble your heart and accept that God loves you more than you can ever understand. Frankly, we'll never understand everything in these finite bodies. What we can understand, though, is that Jesus is real, He loves you, and He died on that cross with you in mind.

I HOPE you'll pray the following prayer with me:

"Lord soften my heart, open my eyes and take my hand I pray. Lead me to understanding and to a place of humility. Your grace is sufficient, your love is abounding, your power is overwhelming, and your name is Holy. I ask for your forgiveness and I thank you for your sacrifice. Come into my life. Fill my heart with your Holy Spirit oh God and show me the life you've designed for me. Let me experience your presence Lord and please show me the truth. Show me who Jesus IS. Show me who you ARE."

YOU ARE LOVED.

RESOURCES

To ensure that you have the complete and updated list, please email **contact@jpmihail.com** for a PDF with clickable links to these books and resources.

For further association and connection, please request to join the private Facebook community group called: <u>**Pursuing Truth & Finding Jesus Community**</u>

BOOKS:

1. *A Study Bible* (NKJV, ESV and ASV are my recommended translations to start)
2. *Extreme Devotion* - The Voice of the Martyrs
3. *Mere Christianity* - C.S. Lewis
4. *The Pilgrim's Progress* - John Bunyan
5. *The Case for Christ: A Journalist's Personal Investigation of the Evidence for Jesus* - Lee Strobel
6. *More Than a Carpenter* - Josh & Sean McDowell
7. *I Don't Have Enough Faith to be an Atheist* - Norman Geisler & Frank Turek
8. *Stealing from God: Why Atheists Need God to Make Their Case* - Frank Turek
9. *Wild at Heart: Discovering the Secrets of a Man's Soul* - John Eldrege
10. *Captivating: Unveiling the Mystery of a Woman's Soul* - John & Stasi Eldredge
11. *Priceless: A Woman to be Praised* - Billie Kaye Tsika
12. *Get Married, Stay Married* - Paul & Billie Kaye Tsika
13. *Finally Free* - Heath Lambert

MOVIES/TV:

1. The Case for Christ (2017)
2. The Passion of the Christ (2004)
3. The Gospel of John (2003)
4. Paul, Apostle of Christ (2018)
5. Unplanned (2019)
6. The Chosen TV Series (2017 - present)
7. The Bible TV Series (2013)

YouTube Channels/Podcasts:

1. The Bible Project
2. Cross Examined
3. Real Life with Jack Hibbs
4. Real Faith with Mark Driscoll
5. Living Waters
6. Grace to You with John MacArthur
7. Acts 17 Apologetics
8. The Ten Minute Bible Hour
9. Mike Winger
10. In Touch Ministries with Dr. Charles Stanley

Other Speakers/Authors:

1. Dr. William Laine Craig
2. J. Warner Wallace
3. C.S. Lewis
4. Nabeel Qureshi
5. J.D. Farag
6. John Piper
7. Chuck Swindoll
8. Kent Hovind
9. Ken Ham

NOTES

1. Michelangelo. (n.d.-b). The Creation of Adam [Painting]. In https://www.michelangelo.org/the-creation-of-adam.jsp

2. Lewis, C. S. (n.d.). A quote by C.S. Lewis. Goodreads. Retrieved February 6, 2021, from https://www.goodreads.com/quotes/26465-christianity-if-false-is-of-no-importance-and-if-true

3. National Fatherhood Initiative. (2020). The Proof is in: Father Absence Harms Children [Illustration]. Fatherhood.Org. https://www.fatherhood.org/father-absence-statistic

4. MADD. (n.d.). History. Retrieved

February 5, 2021, from https://www.madd.org/history/

5. Elite Driving School. (2020). MADD History Impact of Mothers Against Drunk Driving. https://drivingschool.net/madd-history-impact-mothers-drunk-driving/

6. Stewart, R. B. (n.d.). C.S. Lewis' Journey to Faith. CBN.Com. Retrieved February 6, 2021, from https://www1.cbn.com/cs-lewis-journey-faith

7. Carter, J. (2017, October 31). 9 Things You Should Know About J. R. R. Tolkien. The Gospel Coalition. https://www.thegospelcoalition.org/article/9-things-you-should-know-about-j-r-r-tolkien/

8. Geiger, B. (2019, November 11). Explainer: Earth — layer by layer. Science News for Students. https://www.sciencenewsforstudents.org/article/explainer-earth-layer-layer

9. Coolman, R. (2014, May 12). Keeping Time: The Origin of B.C. & A.D. Livescience.Com. https://www.livescience.com/45510-anno-domini.html